DESIGN
INSPIRATIONS

VOLUME I

DESIGN
INSPIRATIONS

VOLUME I

CHARLOTTE MOSS

WRITTEN WITH JENNIFER CEGIELSKI

DESIGN BY DINA DELL'ARCIPRETE, dk DESIGN PARTNERS INC, NYC

CONTENTS

INTRODUCTION

" Inspiration starts with observation.
Once you look at the world we live in, you'll
be able to create a world in which to live. **"**

—CHARLOTTE MOSS

I am often asked the question "What inspires you?" In all the lectures and interviews I give, the people I meet never seem to tire of wanting to know where the ideas for designing a room come from, or where to begin when starting a design process for their own homes. I've been in the decorating business now for almost twenty years, and I've decided that maybe the best way to answer this question is to revisit the archive of my work and share examples of rooms I've created and discuss how each came to be. The result is this book—the first in a series—which tells the story behind the story of four rooms I created for decorator show houses.

For those who may not be familiar with the concept, a show house is a collaboration for a good cause. A selection of reputable decorators are invited to participate, and the different rooms within the location are allotted or awarded to them. After that, it is up to the decorators to work some magic and come up with plans to fully furnish the rooms with the cooperation of fabric houses, antiques dealers, fixtures suppliers, and others in the industry. Tickets to view the house are sold to the public to benefit a specific charity, but it's a win-win situation for everyone involved: decorators are able to experiment with concepts they have been wanting to try and create a fantasy environment unconstrained by a client's wishes or demands; suppliers and dealers have the opportunity to display new collections and inventory; and viewers new and old to decorating get to soak up as many ideas as they can for a nominal fee.

I have participated in more than a dozen show houses, and have chosen for this book three examples of rooms from Kips Bay Show Houses and one from a French Decorator Show House, all of which were in New York. The Kips Bay Decorator Show House is one of the most well known; it benefits the Kips Bay Boys & Girls Club, which since 1915 has enriched the lives of nearly nine thousand children in the Bronx as a nurturing environment for study, recreation, and making friends. In the French Designer Show House, rooms are interpreted in *le style français* for the benefit of the American Hospital of Paris, which is located on the site of one of Louis XV's summer homes in Neuilly-sur-Seine and has offered American-style medicine for more than eighty five years. I am proud and privileged to have been a part of these wonderful show houses.

In addition to my discussion of the four show house rooms, you'll find a few apropos quotes about inspiration sprinkled throughout these pages. I'm a collector of quotes, particularly from people whose lives or work I admire. One of my favorites is by the photographer Walker Evans, who advised his students, "Stare. It is the way to educate your eye, and more." Obviously, this is important advice for fellow photographers, but I think that what Mr. Evans said really applies to most creative endeavors, decorating included. This looking, observing, and really *seeing* things around you broadens your knowledge base so that you can create the environment you've always wanted. Looking doesn't cost anything, and it's something most people can do, easily and wherever they are. Think of it as going through life as a big sponge, soaking up ideas as you find them!

I believe we derive inspiration from the things we see and experience that strike a chord with us and stay with us for a long time. One little memory or moment in your collective unconscious may be a great source of inspiration when you are decorating your home. An image, a color, or an object you encounter while visiting a museum, traveling, or even walking your dog down the street could become part of a great decorating idea later. I find inspiration in many places: through the imagery and craftsmanship of art, architecture, fashion, photography, and individual objects; through color and the natural beauty of flowers, plants, and gardens; and through the books I read and my own experiences while on my travels and when building my collections. I am also inspired by women through the ages who had a sense of humor and great personal style. All these things I keep in the back of my mind for future use.

When something strikes me, I like to record it in some way to jog my memory later. I have a huge archive of images and tear sheets that I store in thematic portfolios. You might say I'm an incurable clipper! These resources come in handy when I'm presenting a scheme for a room. I always revisit my scrapbooks and files and assemble an inspiration board with a selection of pictures, sketches, postcards, tear sheets, fabric swatches, and quotes to convey a sense of mood and atmosphere for my clients in order to help them visualize my concept. You'll see examples of my own inspiration boards, as well as room schemes, in each chapter.

So what advice can I offer someone in search of inspiration? Go out, go do, go see. Take lots of photographs, and keep scrapbooks or start an inspiration board. Browse the home shops, visit museums and exhibitions, attend lectures, antiques shows, and, of course, show houses. Read books and magazines about interiors; look carefully at their pictures and think to yourself, What is it that I really like about this room—is it the color, is it the detail, is it the floor plan, is it one great chair? From all this looking, you can learn to take concepts and make them work for you and your home. The best homes are personal homes, places that have "fingerprints." Choose furniture and objects not just because they look pretty but because they elicit an emotional response. If you like something, it will always have a home. You'll find that your inspiration just clicks—when you're not even thinking about it, things will just seem to come together. The beauty of this is that each of us has a different way of extracting knowledge, and everybody can see something different in the same thing. I hope you'll be inspired by what you see on these pages.

A FEMININE RETREAT

A SUMPTUOUS TOILE WITH A VENETIAN THEME, THE NOTION OF A GARDEN FOLLY,
AND ARTFUL ILLUSIONS RESULT IN A COZY FANTASY HIDEAWAY
DESIGNED FOR WRITING AND DREAMING

I can't resist a good folly. Not a folly in the sense of a doomed undertaking or an old-time theatrical review—no, the type of folly I'm talking about is a *maison de plaisance,* those fanciful gazebos, grottoes, pavilions, and small-scale buildings found in the gardens of magnificent palaces throughout the Continent. I've seen many such structures on my travels, and I love them because they are designed solely for pleasure and because they are often created with an amusing twist, be it some fantasy artifice or playful illusion. When it came time to transform a diminutive passageway in a Kips Bay Show House into a usable room, I seized upon the opportunity to concoct a sort of illusion-infused folly of my own, complete with a faux window overlooking an imagined landscape.

To say the room was small is an understatement—the area measured a mere five by twelve feet, to be exact. As I am often asked for advice on decorating in close quarters, I relished the challenge this room presented. It made sense to me that a chamber of this size should serve as an intimate retreat for a lady, a "room of one's own" with a place to write and a nook for lounging. To make the most of the space, I closed off a pair of French doors and made a wall (this became the area at the back of the bed). I also closed two other doors on the right side of the room and concealed them with a fabric-covered screen. You might have thought that someone was dressing behind it—further fuel for the folly!

While developing a scheme for the room, I came across this particular Venetian-themed toile de Jouy. Toile is one of my favorite fabrics, because it always tells a little story to those who look closely. In this case, the story is one of carefree enjoyment and leisure—the characters are painting, fishing, and lazily drifting along in a gondola in a beautiful natural setting. Clearly, the fabric became the most important ingredient in this room. In using one single fabric in abundance, the goal was to trick the eye into making a small space look larger—you might think of it as trompe l'oeil decorating.

Small rooms really can accommodate only a small selection of furniture, and this room was no exception. A grand wall-to-wall daybed at one end of the space would be the main focus. With the underlying Venetian theme in mind, I recalled an eighteenth-century engraving I have of a *lit à la Turque*, or Turkish bed. The canopy of the bed reminded me of the awnings you might see gracing elegant Venetian palazzos, and I sought to give the valance on this bed a similar shape. I often find that it's these little details in a work of art that catch my eye and inspire me later. Beyond the bed, just two or three additional pieces were possible, so of course they had to be fabulous. My favorite is an elegant writing table originally owned by the renowned decorator Elsie de Wolfe; it fit into the space so perfectly. Similarly, when you are decorating a room of your own, determine the most important piece of furniture you absolutely need for the room to function and buy the best you can. Then let the decorating process develop and proceed slowly around this piece.

When I saw a serendipitous folly depicted in toile, I instantly knew that I had to use this fabric for this room. If you look carefully you'll see a suitor wooing a lady—even the squirrels are having a good time scampering about!

" …before I start painting, I reflect, I dream. **"** —BONNARD

16

THE INSPIRATION

From the magical city of
Venice to the great gardens
of Europe, the wonderful
places I've visited have been
a definite inspiration. This
board is composed of sou-
venir postcards of paintings
of the Grand Canal and
photographs of follies, such
as the tower I climbed at
Chanteloup in the Loire
Valley (right, center) and
the hedge maze in the
garden at Woburn Abbey
(right, corner), as well as
fabric remnants and tear
sheets of furniture, rooms,
and works of art I admired.
My quest for pagodas led
me to create my own
(center, top) in conjunction
with decorating resource
Niermann Weeks; it also
serves as a tulipiere for
fresh flowers.

A GARDEN FANTASY

The entryway to the room was
at the top of a landing. I wanted
the entire space to capture the
feeling of a garden folly and give
a sense of the outside coming in,
so we installed a window-box
planter of boxwood along the
stairway railing and added treillage walls and an urn by Bertrand
Servenay. The settee provides the
perfect trysting spot!

THE SCHEME

The fabric was the driving force behind assembling the other elements. As toiles go, this was a very unusual example; most are printed using one or two colors on a solid ground, but this toile was created with twelve shades of a single color. The lovely mix of sepia and café au lait made it look almost like an engraving—the palette created drama, while the print introduced a sense of playful ease to the room. Formal, but fun! After that, everything else fell into place: the rich solid-colored accent silks, the amazing vintage trim I found in Paris with gold filament acorns, golden oak leaf charms, and—in a nod to the Venetian theme—luxurious Fortuny tassels.

In addition to Elsie de Wolfe's writing desk, I'm thrilled to have in my collection her personal photo album as well. Many of the images were taken by the legendary photographer Baron Adolf de Meyer. The photograph of Elsie posing near a rose arbor (above) inspired me to create a garden feeling for the entry to the room.

The faux window with mirrored glass panes above the desk (opposite) served several purposes—first, to encourage the illusion that someone could sit at the desk and enjoy the view, thereby creating a sense of spaciousness in the room; second, to create a break for the eye as it gazes around the room, since the fabric covers the entire surrounding area; and third, to help reflect some light around an otherwise dim space. Meanwhile, an electrical panel was camouflaged behind the drapery of the window. And, just for fun, we penned a letter from Marie Antoinette to her mother and left it on the desk. This copy of an antique wallpaper by Zuber et Cie (above) along the stairway helped set the playful mood by greeting visitors with assorted Chinese characters dancing in the landscape.

"DRIFT, DREAM, DELIGHT, DECORATE..."

—Charlotte Moss

Pagoda motifs and chinoiserie in general always seem to work their way into my designs somehow. I snapped this magnificent folly in a garden near Naples, Italy, while on my travels. Who would have thought the Neapolitans shared my passion for pagodas with such gusto?

A COUNTESS'S CHAMBER

A PHOTOGRAPH OF AN UNFORGETTABLE BED IN A COUNTESS'S VILLA
AND A FORTUITOUS COLLABORATION INSPIRED A RELAXED, LUXURIOUS SETTING
THAT CONJURES UP VISIONS OF A FAR-OFF EXOTIC LOCALE

I have a keen appreciation for fashion history, which seems to have manifested itself in the numerous volumes I've collected on the topic. The books are often favorite sources of inspiration, and one in particular packed a trifecta-punch when it came to the decor of a show house. The seed for the vision of this room was planted while I was reading *Mona Bismarck, Balenciaga, Cecil Beaton*. Mona Bismarck was a Southern socialite and one of the most elegant women of her time. She served as muse for the Spanish fashion designer Cristobal Balenciaga, a master of the art of couture. The inimitable Cecil Beaton is probably best remembered for his photographs of cultural icons, artistic figures, and royalty, even though his wonderful talents extended into other areas, such as painting. To begin, all three are characters I admire for various reasons. I find women like Mona endlessly intriguing, and I have a number of Balenciaga's couture pieces, as well as a selection of Beaton's books, photographs, and watercolors. Furthermore, their collaborations strike a chord with me, because decorating is also about collaborating. As a decorator you must ask a lot of personal questions, get answers, and learn how to interpret those answers in order to achieve the best results.

Now, it was in this book about these fascinating people that I saw a photograph of a one-of-a-kind bed that Mona had in a guest room in her villa on the island of Capri. The bed was Venetian with chinoiserie decoration, and it sprouted a single fanciful umbrella at its head. When the opportunity arose to design a room for a Kips Bay show house, I immediately remembered Mona's bed. I envisioned a room for relaxing and reading, with an atmosphere that could transport the visitor somewhere far and away—to say a houseboat in India, say, or a beach in the Seychelles.

I went on a mad search to find somebody who could re-create this bed. The original had a curved wooden headboard that would have taken a long time to make. We had only thirty days, and nobody would consider it. Then I visited antiques dealer Tony Victoria at his atelier. I showed him the photograph and my sketches and explained what I wanted to do. Not only was Tony game for my creation but, as luck would have it, he had squirreled away in his storage room two tole umbrellas that his father had bought a long time ago. He thought the umbrellas probably came from India, where they would have been used on a sedan chair atop an elephant. In a moment of design serendipity, I was convinced that these umbrellas had been waiting for me and, though the original design had only one, I decided to incorporate both of these beauties.

In the finished product, the umbrellas are at an angle to suggest a sea breeze, and the cache of pillows on the bed conveys a relaxed, luxurious mood. These pillows were made from small pieces of fabric remnants. I recommend collecting and using fabrics you like, and mixing things up a bit. I have paired embroidered Chinese fabrics and leopard-skin prints here—visible proof that patterns *do not* have to match!

Antiques dealer Tony Victoria already had the tole umbrellas as well as a pair of tall posts carved like palm trees in his atelier, so all we needed to do was craft arms to keep the umbrellas balanced and assemble all the pieces.

THE INSPIRATION

It is clear that I have no shortage of scrapbook images of fashionable women, chinoiserie, or, it seems, umbrellas! This assemblage includes a photograph of Mona's original bed (left, center) and my sketch for my two-umbrella reproduction (right, center), as well as a photo of one of the umbrellas we used in its original state when Tony unearthed it (right, top corner). You'll also find umbrella themes ranging from a hand-colored eighteenth-century engraving of a man in a sled (right, bottom) to fashion photos by Lartigue (right, center) and Horst (right, bottom). I never miss a chance to visit a museum shop. The postcards they sell (left, bottom) make inexpensive souvenirs, and I always buy extras for reference and to write notes or wrap in a pretty ribbon to give as a gift.

BALENCIAGA

Rizzoli

" ...all you have to do is drift away into a dream
to find inspiration. " —GAUGUIN

COMFORT AND CONVERSATION

I envisioned this boudoir as a place to receive visitors or somewhere to simply relax and read a book or enjoy a cup of tea as well as the peace and quiet. Overall there is a very natural theme to the room, from the flora and fauna on the wall panels and botanical images on the chinoiserie cushions and Aubusson rugs to the porcelain melons created by Lady Anne Gordon and the bowl of exotic fruits along the back wall. Two pieces of furniture are of note. The chair with the heart-shaped back is known as a *fauteuil de coiffeur* due to its function—the way the back curves down at the top allowed ladies to have their hair done while sitting in the chair. Directly in front of the sofa is a side table that Syrie Maugham made for the Duchess of Windsor (also a client of Balenciaga); I repurposed the piece as a petite coffee table, because its stepped shelves cleverly keep notes, journals, or your latest book close at hand.

" I DON'T WANT TO BE

REASONABLE—

THERE'S PLENTY OF TIME FOR

THAT IN THE GRAVE.

WHAT I WANT IS ADVENTURE,

INNOVATION, FOOLISHNESS

AND DISCOVERY. "

—Mirabel Osler, *A Breath from Elsewhere*

This photograph was taken by Gleb Derujinsky, who pioneered the practice of shooting fashion stories on location throughout the world in the 1950s. For me, the image kind of sums it all up—a gorgeously dressed woman (in this case, Derujinsky's wife, the model Ruth Neumann), an umbrella, an exotic locale. Heaven!

I believe that in addition to being a useful place to pay bills or write letters, a workspace should be physically comfortable and visually exciting. The tonal pink and white palette imbues this anteroom (opposite) with a soothing quality, while the leopard footstool offers comfort with a dash of humor. The series of eighteenth-century French fashion engravings on the wall were particularly inspiring, as each one had so much detail; I liked the idea of taking different examples of a single subject and framing them all the same way, then spacing them to give the impression of an important collection or one big work of art. The gilded jardiniere on top of the secretaire (above) encourages the eye to travel upward in the room. Though this isn't the usual place for a planter, it adds interest to the room as well as balancing out the grid of engravings. The sunburst mirror behind it brightens the back wall.

THE SCHEME

The amazing hand-painted
De Gournay wall panels
create an overall feeling of
green in the background,
which was then echoed by the
colors of the Aubusson rug
and the green velvet sofa. The
effect was tonal, punched up
with jolts of color by such
accessories as this porcelain
melon (left corner). Silks
from old Chinese robes (far
left and far right) added a
layer of richness.

In this seating area of the room, you might entertain a friend or two. The tufted sofa is a cozy place to have a pot of tea and a chat, and the *fauteuil de coiffeur* and caned chair are easy to move in closer should a larger group come to call. On the coffee table is a smaller arrangement of poppies derived from the series on the fireplace mantel; their citrusy palette is echoed by the real citrus in the background.

Overleaf: Though framed like a painting, this deceptive artwork is in fact an old panel of French wallpaper featuring a dog and a Chinese tea urn. The image is partially obscured by a random row of poppies of variegated heights. One simple type of blossom can tell the whole story and create drama when massed.

This series of hand-painted De Gournay
wall panels envelop the room and set a
natural scheme by placing the visitor in an
interior landscape. Mona Bismarck inspired
their selection as well—when she was
Mrs. Harrison Williams, Beaton painted a
watercolor of the lady and her husband
sitting on a sofa in Palm Beach, and the
walls of the room in which they were seated
were ornamented with similar panels.

Icelandic poppies and a grouping of precious and not-so-precious vases atop a nineteenth-century Venetian black-amoor table (above) create an unconventional arrangement that greets each visitor to the room. I love the way the poppies' stems twist and curl—their form echoes the fluid movement of the umbrellas on the bed. Another grid of engravings (opposite) with views of French gardens calls to mind the series adjacent to the secretaire. Their graphic black-and-white imagery is a welcome break for the eye against an already colorful wall.

It's no secret that I love lacquered furniture and accessories—at least one piece appears in nearly every room I decorate! Case in point: the magnificent William & Mary chest (opposite) and the miniature folding screen with hand-painted panels (above) atop the Louis XV commode. I'm especially responsive to the feeling of lacquer and the way you can see the layers. And of course I can't resist how the chinoiserie figures and landscapes found on lacquered pieces tell a story, much like the characters on toile de Jouy. With some of the larger pieces, you run the risk of creating a flat symmetrical line in the room that ends at the top of the piece. To counteract this, a grouping of objects of various heights (such as the vases shown opposite) can help extend the eye upward.

"WE DON'T CREATE, WE JUST ASSEMBLE—IT'S ALREADY THERE."

— George Balanchine

I have several eighteenth-century furniture engravings in my collection, but what I love about this one in particular is how it dissects a French settee into a series of parts to illustrate how the whole piece is composed.

Pl. 7.

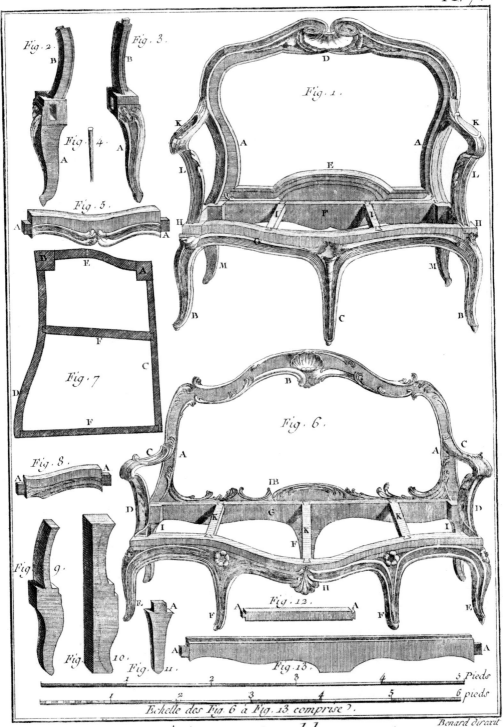

Fig. 2. Fig. 3. Fig. 4. Fig. 5. Fig. 7. Fig. 8. Fig. 9. Fig. 10. Fig. 11. Fig. 1. Fig. 6. Fig. 12. Fig. 13.

5 Pieds

6 pieds

Echelle des Fig. 6 à Fig. 13 comprise.

Benard direxit.

Menuisier en Meubles, Canapés.

A BLISSFUL BEDROOM

THE DISCOVERY OF AN ENCHANTING DOCUMENT FABRIC AND THE QUEST
FOR A DISTINCTIVE BED LED TO THE CREATION OF AN ELEGANT BLOSSOM-STREWN
BEDROOM TO SOOTHE THE SOUL

Being in the decorating business, I have the luxury of viewing hundreds—maybe even thousands!—of fabrics from the top houses every year. Every once in a while I stumble upon a particularly wonderful design that ends up as the basis of an entire room. So it was with the incredible floral document fabric you see here, which I first saw while working on a design project with the talented folks from Colonial Williamsburg. In addition to its eminent standing as a historic site, Williamsburg has an amazing collection of document fabrics in its holdings (which makes it a national treasure in my book). The Williamsburg foundation often partners with the great fabric houses and chooses a selection of fabrics from an archive of thousands of designs to reproduce for its special Reserve Collection.

In any event, one night after a long day's work, one of the ladies I was with asked me if I wanted to see the fabrics that were going to be released for the next season. A sneak peek? She didn't have to ask twice! I looked through boxes and boxes of new fabrics and stopped when I found "Palampore Border." I had already committed to participating in the French Designer Show House, and right then and there I knew that this one irresistible fabric was going to be the main story of the room I planned to do. Simply put, it just looked French; its red-and-blue palette reminded me of French Provincial fabrics, and though the original document currently resides in Williamsburg, it could very well have had its origins in France.

As my decorating style has a somewhat French accent, this particular show house gave me an opportunity to decorate not only *à la française* but *pour moi*! So while the fabric would also have worked just as well in other types of rooms, I ultimately decided to use it in a bedroom setting, since I had already designed a living room, a library, a dining room, and several spaces for women in previous show houses. I set out to create a place that was not just somewhere to sleep (although that also played a major role, as you will see) but a relaxing haven that reflected all my personal interests: reading, collecting, writing letters, and planning entertainments for friends and improvements for the garden. I wanted to make sure there was ample space designated for reading and writing, even if the bed was the focus of the room.

As chance would have it, I had recently commissioned a *lit à la Polonaise* for my home in New York. In the eighteenth century, this regally crowned version of the canopied bed had occupied salon-like bedrooms where aristocrats and royals held court in their nightclothes. I have slept in beds of this style while on my travels, and I love the feeling of being in a "room within a room" beneath their canopies. They are the perfect bed for drifting off into your dreams—asleep or awake! Since I had already planned to feature a grand bed in this show house, I thought why not use my bed there first? The document fabric would upholster the bed, as well as the walls, to create a room that completely envelops you.

While I always like to put fresh flowers in my rooms, this little bedside arrangement seemed particularly appropriate here because of the floral theme set by the document fabric. The antique tole vase holds a handful of garden roses and scented geranium; their fragrance perfumes the room.

> **"A woman's environment will speak for her life, whether she likes it or not."** —ELSIE DE WOLFE

THE INSPIRATION

I envisioned this as a room
for women with great style,
accomplishment, and per-
sonality. Inspiring images of
such women include the chic
mannequins in fashion illus-
trations by Balenciaga (left,
bottom) and Ruben Toledo
(right, top), the model
Carmen with a leopard in a
black-and-white Derujinsky
photo (left, corner), Elsie
de Wolfe captured in a shot
from her younger years
(right, bottom), and a very
sassy Ella Fitzgerald (right,
center) in a postcard of an
Annie Leibovitz photo. Also
tacked to this particular
board are assorted museum
postcards and travel photographs: a Sevres porcelain
floral arrangement (left,
top), period shoes (right,
center), and snapshots from
Williamsburg and Versailles
(center, bottom).

RELAX AND UNWIND   I believe the bedroom should be a retreat, with no homework and no computers, so that you can completely relax without any distraction. All the things you may need—your books in progress, a carafe of water or a pot of tea, a journal—should be close at hand. For me, the ultimate fantasy is settling in with a fully stocked bed tray on a Saturday morning (below), with the dogs at the foot of the bed, a cup of coffee, and all the magazines and newspapers I want to peruse. A good-sized table next to the bed (opposite) controls any overflow. While I'm charmed by its very existence, the child-size chair I tucked beneath the painted table here serves two purposes as well: it fills a void under the table and creates a sense of elevation and mass, and it is a useful little storage spot for a stack of books. A basket like the one underneath the console on page 82 would also do the trick.

The most blissful bedrooms
deliver you to dreams even be-
fore you fall asleep, and no piece
of furniture has the power to
transport quite like the *lit à la
Polonaise*. This bed is, of course,
the centerpiece of the room. Its
size means there is no denying
the fact that this is a place for
sleeping, but the room is also a
calm haven from the rest of the
world. With its frame festooned
with the blossom-strewn fabric,
the bed turns into a bower of
sorts. The canopy is lined with a
coral-colored fabric in a tiny print
that is also from the Colonial
Williamsburg Reserve Collection.
When you enter the room, you
look right across the bed to see
the nineteenth-century lacquer
cabinet in the corner; the eye
is drawn upward because of
the height of the bed and the
surrounding furniture. The cabinet
and other lacquered pieces add
touches of black to contrast with
the sweetness of the overall
palette; their strong, vertical lines
counterbalance all the blossoming
swirls of the pattern.

"LIKE A JEWEL NESTLED IN A VELVET-LINED BOX, A BED LIKE THIS IS LIKE A ROOM INSIDE A ROOM. A MYSTERIOUS AND COZY COCOON FLOATING OFF TO ANYWHERE...AND MAYBE NOWHERE."

—Charlotte Moss

I had the pleasure of sleeping in this incredible lit à la Polonaise *while visiting* Château Bagnols *in France. Positioned in the center of the room, the bed practically floated! Its style certainly made an impact on the type of bed I chose to feature in the French Designer Show House.*

THE SCHEME

*The coral-colored fern pattern
(far left) serves as the lining
for the main floral. When you
put two patterns together,
make sure they are good
partners and don't compete.
You can do this by relating
their palettes or part of their
palettes, choosing an overall
theme, or by playing with
scale, such as pairing a little
print with a big one, as I did
here, for example. I always
think it works better when
something is just a little bit off,
a successful mix rather than a
perfect match. If you can't
commit to using pattern in a
major way on furniture or cur-
tains, play it safe with something small (such as a pillow
or a lampshade). I also like to
suggest looking beyond a pattern's uses in its "as-is" state;
for instance, if your fabric has
a printed border, why not cut it
off and use it where you want
to? I did just that with this
border—look for it throughout
the room as trim running
along the top of the chair rail
and also along the valance on
the curtain. You might do
something similar to embellish
a bed skirt, a pillow, or a box
cushion. The fabric trims itself!*

In this room, the painted fireplace is flanked by two "activity areas" where reading and writing could take place; the latter appears here (opposite). In homage to fashion's inspiration, a black-and-white photograph of the innovative designer Claire McCardell presides over the Louis XV mahogany desk and a selection of fashion books sit in a come-what-may stack against the fireplace column. Don't fret that all your possessions have to be really ordered; a few casual arrangements of your favorite things or your latest obsession create a relaxed atmosphere and make your home look inhabited. As the decorator Madeleine Castaing once quipped, "Do you understand, *ma chérie,* that perfection can ruin a decor?" I commissioned the pair of maintenance-free potted tole dahlias (left and above) especially for this room. More objects than true botanical elements, they take the blooms on the walls to a third dimension as well as help guide the eye upward in the room.

To the left of the fireplace is the reading corner. I purposely chose to slipcover the chair (opposite) so that it would feel a bit loose in contrast with the rest of the upholstery in the room. The standing lamp offers a place to rest a cup of tea within arm's reach; its zingy red shade does so much more for the room than a white lampshade ever could. Strategic bits of color really bring a room together. That being said, black is also important here. The black lacquer of the little bookcase and other furniture is echoed by the artwork, which includes eighteenth-century engravings of Versailles and Marly (opposite) and a sketch of a Dior skirt by René Bouché (above). The upholstered walls really are the color, so I wanted all the art to be in graphic black and white. Ultimately, what makes a room feel rich is that intriguing mix of things from different periods and places. The three blue-and-white Delft vases clustered asymmetrically on top of the cabinet create a modern positioning of porcelain.

" THOUGHTFUL DECISIONS ARE THE RESULT OF A FOCUSED APPROACH. IN DECORATING THIS APPROACH IS A PROCESS, DO YOURSELF A FAVOR AND FOLLOW THESE FIVE STEPS: FANTASIZE, ANALYZE, VISUALIZE, OBSERVE, REALIZE. "

—Charlotte Moss, *Creating a Room*

I visited this pavilion in the gardens of Villandry in France. It inspired the fantasy house in my head—a petite château filled with tubs of mock orange and jasmine trees. I'd have a lit à la Polonaise floating in the middle of a book-lined room with limestone floors and a cozy fire, and I'd enjoy the company of my dogs while taking in the view of a canal lined with a pleached hornbeam hedge underplanted with lavender.

A ROOM FOR CONVERSATION

AN ARTIST'S WORK INSPIRES AN ENTIRE COLOR PALETTE AND A
TECHNIQUE OF DECORATING THE WAY A COUTURIER APPROACHES FASHION
RESULTS IN A ROOM MADE FOR DIALOGUE AND DISCUSSION

I think people who decorate always carry around ideas for rooms in their heads.
I know I do. There is always a fabric, a scheme, a particular piece of furniture, or something else I love, but the right opportunity to use it hasn't presented itself. In the case
of this room, it was all about color for me. As you may or may not know, I am not from
the beige school of decorating. I have never even gone through a "beige phase"; color
has always played a very prominent role in my work. This room is no exception, but
I wanted to approach color in a slightly different way. On a trip to Madrid, I was
looking at a room filled with Goya's paintings in the Prado Museum when I saw how
he paired the pinks with the melons, the blue aqua skies and the toasty browns. It was
a palette that I couldn't wait to work with, and a new Kips Bay Show House was the
perfect place to experiment. I planned to start with a neutral ground of bronze and
brown, and punctuate it with blocks of color—deep pink, mango, and aqua from
Goya's haunting palette. On a separate occasion I saw a work by Helen Frankenthaler
with strokes of pink, brown, and ivory. Unlike a realistic painting with heavy details,
it conveyed feeling through technique and color. After that, a scheme started evolving
which ultimately translated into "A Room for Conversation." This is a room for girls,
but gentlemen are invited.

Decorating, after all, is about making a room look as good as possible, rather like clothes and fashion. As a matter of principle, I think all good rooms are created the way a couturier puts an ensemble together. The bones are the architecture, and the furnishings are added one layer at a time like clothing and accessories, with a plan and a vision for the finished look. Here, the bones formed a square room anchored by a fireplace at one end. The problem is that where there's a fireplace, there's not only a fire but people who tend to congregate by it. With conversation as the goal, it was important to get the balance of the furniture and the layout of the room right in order to put people in close proximity and encourage interaction without everyone ending up on one side of the room. The weight and location of the fireplace required that a balance be created for the opposite side, where there was a little shallow niche in the wall that I thought would be nice filled with a screen. I chose a coromandel screen and a Jansen-style sofa banquette, which fit in front of the screen perfectly. Add a few chairs that are easily moved around, and you can accommodate different occasions or larger groups of people.

Another link this room has with fashion is skirts—or, more accurately, the lack thereof. None of the upholstered furniture has a skirt, and I think this was the first time I had ever done a room where all the legs were on show. The room has a lightness and openness, and since it is all about conversation and moving around, perhaps my decorating instinct informed me that if there were skirts down to the floor the room would not have had such flexibility.

For the window panels, I wanted something with a textural quality that wouldn't add too much pattern to the room. I built upon an already wonderful fabric with custom silk-screening—the pattern created a tonal design. In lieu of elaborate passementerie, the panels were trimmed with a strip of pink faille and tobacco raw-silk welting.

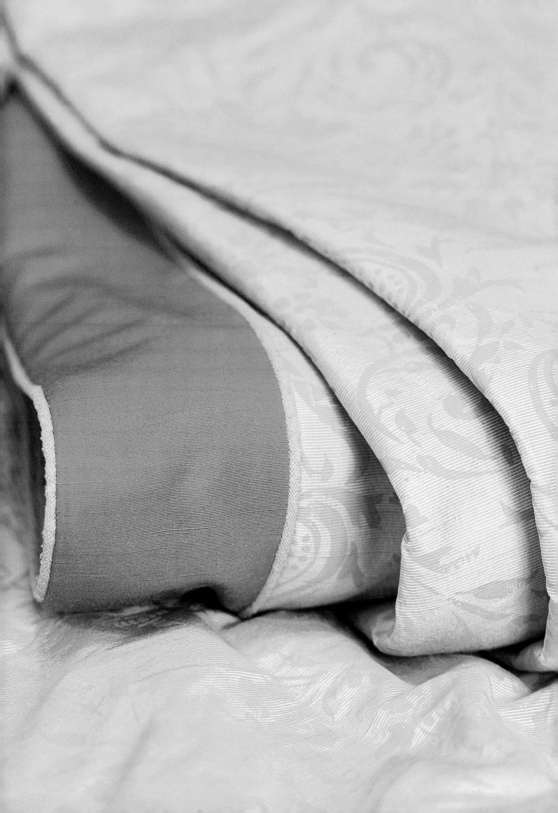

THE INSPIRATION

*In thinking about the
ambience of a room for
conversation, I pictured
the glamour and charming
repartee of a 1940s salon.
A Rex Whistler drawing
entitled, appropriately
enough, "The Conversation"
(right, corner) further
encouraged this fantasy
concept, with its depiction
of a mixed group of men
and women. This board is
also composed of travel
photos from my trip to
Spain (left, top), assorted
Goya paintings (left and
right, center), a picture of
a Chinese screen that
now resides in my office
(center, top), examples of
low seating (right, top and
bottom), as well as a photo
of Madame Chanel (center,
bottom), whose own sofa
in her apartment above her
shop on the Rue Cambon
was similar to the one I
selected for this room.*

“A great ambiance is greater than the sum of its parts.”

—TONY DUQUETTE

HIGH AND LOW I mean this in both the literal and the figurative sense. Literally, the eye is drawn high in the room by the artwork above the fireplace on the other side of the room and by the top of the coromandel screen. The eye is also cast downward to the pair of slipper chairs (opposite). I must confess—I borrowed the low-seating concept from the 1940s Hollywood decorator Billy Haines, who slung chairs extra low to make the sitters' legs look extra long. He believed these chairs flattered everyone. And, by the way, not every item in a room need be expensive to look great—it's perfectly acceptable to mix "dime store with couture." Take, for example, the cushions on the banquette—they each cost less than $30. With a little innovation, you can even transform an affordable chair into something special. These languid beauties from Crate & Barrel were recovered in pink leather flipped to the sueded side and gauffraged. At the other end of the spectrum is the luxurious lippy cat throw made for me by Dennis Basso; it is banded and backed with a delicious layer of petal-pink cashmere.

THE SCHEME

Interestingly, this room took on a secondary palette, as shown by this scheme composed for the seating area in front of the fireplace. The antiqued velvet and the plaid were used to upholster my "Sybaritic chair," while the bold botanical was put into use on the Swedish-style chair. The rose quartz used in the glass vases to anchor the stems of dogwood gave a nod to the pink accents in the other portion of the room, while a Matisse drawing (top left) evoked that feeling of a lively Parisian salon filled with art and discussion. I imagined the scent from the antique perfume burner (lower right) drifting through the air.

It was logical to place two chairs (opposite) in front of the fireplace along with an ottoman that could be used for extra seating. The chairs are presided over by the Frankenthaler painting, which, in addition to physically being opposite the coromandel screen, is also thematically the polar opposite of the screen's painstakingly detailed imagery. The painting's pink coloration is echoed by the dogwood blossoms in the corner of the room. Flowers are a good way to experiment with small doses of saturated color. It isn't necessary to order an arrangement from the florist; simply take one flower variety and mass it in a vase for something simple and chic. My favorite piece of furniture in this room is the "Sybaritic chair" (opposite, right), my adaptation of a chair owned by Voltaire that I first saw in Paris in the Musee Carnavalet; you can learn more about this chair on the following pages. The pattern on the painted Swedish-style chair (below) is the boldest in the room, and keeps the room from feeling static.

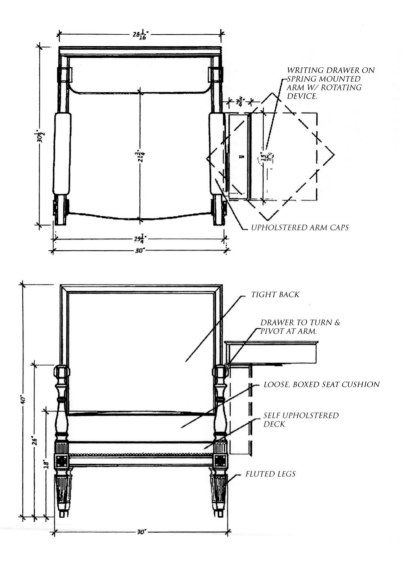

WRITING DRAWER ON
SPRING MOUNTED
ARM W/ ROTATING
DEVICE.

UPHOLSTERED ARM CAPS

TIGHT BACK

DRAWER TO TURN &
PIVOT AT ARM.

LOOSE, BOXED SEAT CUSHION

SELF UPHOLSTERED
DECK

FLUTED LEGS

THE "SYBARITIC CHAIR": FROM ADAPTATION TO FRUITION The original
version of this chair was owned by the eighteenth-century French writer Voltaire. I thought it was a great concept—
you don't need a separate side table, as it is part of the chair. My interpretation is a classic bergère in walnut with a
rotating arm and a little letterbox bookstand that works as a mini desk to hold papers, a journal, or a book. I call it my
retirement chair! As always, a detailed construction drawing was necessary in order to produce the chair. All par-
ties—furniture maker, upholsterer, and designer—used this as a blueprint. In a nod to French upholstery techniques
and tradition, a contrasting and less expensive fabric was used to back the chair (opposite).

" BUT TO CREATE IS TO MAKE VARIATIONS. OF COURSE, ONE MUST BEGIN BY FINDING SOME ELEMENT, A THEME, A MOTIF, A GUIDELINE AROUND WHICH AN IDEA CAN BE DEVELOPED. "

—Valentino

The natural world never ceases to inspire. I picked up this giant conch shell while vacationing; its creamy pink interior translated into the custom color that ended up on the walls of this room.

ROOM SCHEME DETAILS

SHOW HOUSES

American Hospital of Paris
63 Boulevard Victor Hugo
F 92 200 Neuilly-sur-Seine
Tel. +33(0)1 46 41 25 25
information@ahparis.org
www.american-hospital.org

Kips Bay Boys & Girls Club
200 Lexington Avenue
New York, NY 10016
Tel. 212 213 2800
mailinglist@kipsbay.org
www.kipsbay.org

FABRIC HOUSES
All are to the trade only

Brunschwig & Fils
212 838 7878
www.brunschwig.com

F. Schumacher & Company
800 523 1200
www.fschumacher.com

Holland & Sherry
212 355 6241
www.hollandandsherry.com

Scalamandre
212 980 3888
www.buyhomefurnishings.com

Travers & Co.
212 888 7900
www.traversinc.com

A FEMININE RETREAT

FABRICS

UPHOLSTERY

Bed corona:
Travers & Co./Toile
Venetienne/Beige and Taupe
Lining:
Travers & Co./Sandhurst/Bronze
Trim:
Antique gold rope, small tassels
Headboard, bedcover, bedskirt:
Travers & Co./Toile
Venetienne/Beige and Taupe
Screen:
Travers & Co./Toile
Venetienne/Beige and Taupe
Walls:
Travers & Co./Toile
Venetienne/Beige and Taupe

WINDOW TREATMENTS

Panels:
Travers & Co./Toile
Venetienne/Beige and Taupe

ANTIQUE FURNITURE

Louis XV chair, desk, table:
Frederick P. Victoria & Son
631 537 0496
vicantq@worldnet.att.net
19th-century console:
John Rosselli International
(to the trade only)
212 772 2137

ACCESSORIES

Aubusson carpet:
Stark Carpet
(to the trade only)
212 752 9000
www.dir-dd.com
Brass bouillotte lamp:
Julia Gray (to the trade only)
212 223 4454
www.ejvictor.com
Bronze candlestick:
John Rosselli International
(as above)
Chinoiserie panel:
John Rosselli International
(as above)
Chinoiserie tole lantern:
John Rosselli International
(as above)
Painted mirrors with brackets:
John Rosselli International
(as above)
Reproduction Louis XVI lantern:
Christopher Norman, Inc.
(to the trade only)
212 644 4100
www.christophernorman.com
Sevres-style cachepots:
Julia Gray
(as above)
Silver octagonal mirror:
Frederick P. Victoria & Son
(as above)
Trellis panels:
Treillage
212 535 2288
www.treillageonline.com

A FEMININE RETREAT
ROOM SCHEME DETAILS
(see pages 20 and 21)

1. *Travers & Co./Toile Venetienne/*
   Beige and Taupe
2. *Vintage gold-filament acorn trim*
3. *Vintage Chinese silk embroidered tape*
4. *Silver-plate miniature Versailles*
   tub jardiniere
5. *Brass oak leaf*
6. *Silk Fortuny tassel*
7. *Antique leather-bound miniature book*
8. *Waverly/Country Life Sheer/Linen*
9. *Travers & Co./Sandhurst/Bronze*

A COUNTESS'S CHAMBER

ANTEROOM

FABRICS

WINDOW TREATMENTS
Panels and valance:
F. Schumacher/Williamsburg Garden
Damask/Aqua
Trim:
F. Schumacher/Vendome Tassel
Fringe/Rose & Dove
Window shade:
F. Schumacher/Ravinia Silk
Taffeta/Ecru

ANTIQUE FURNITURE

Garden seat:
John Rosselli International
(as above)

George III writing desk:
John Rosselli International
(as above)
Lacquer table:
John Rosselli International
(as above)
Louis XVI desk:
John Rosselli International
(as above)
From the collection of
Charlotte Moss:
Lattice-back arm chair
Leopard footstool

ACCESSORIES

Gilt planter:
Niermann Weeks
www.niermannweeks
Gilt sunburst mirror:
John Rosselli International
(as above)
Venetian-style tole lantern:
John Rosselli International
(as above)

From the collection of
Charlotte Moss:
Aubusson floral pillow
French porcelain painted cup
Pagoda letter holder
Papier-mâché pen cup

SITTING ROOM

FABRICS
UPHOLSTERY

Sofa:
Schumacher/Antique Strie Velvet
Trim:
Brunschwig & Fils/Aqua Fringe
Cushions:
Vintage blue and mauve Chinese
embroidered silk cushions
Vintage silk moiré cushions
Umbrella bed:
F. Schumacher/Antique Strie Velvet

Skirt:
F. Schumacher/Antique Strie
Velvet/Blue
Decorative pillows:
F. Schumacher/Antique Strie
Velvet /Plum
F. Schumacher/Antique Strie
Velvet/Blue
Printed silk floral chine pillows
Leopard pillow
Wall panels:
De Gournay/Stourhead/Yellow
(44) 20 7823 7316
www.degournay.com

WINDOW TREATMENTS

Panels:
F. Schumacher/Pomegranate
Damask/Rose Dusk
Trim:
F. Schumacher/Vendome Tassel
Fringe/Rose and Dove
Window shade:
F. Schumacher/Ravinia Silk
Taffeta/Ecru

ANTIQUE FURNITURE

Blackamoor table:
Hubert des Forges Antiques
212 744 1857
Caned French chairs:
From the collection of
Charlotte Moss
Fruitwood side table:
John Rosselli International
(as above)
Lacquer chest on stand:
Gerald Bland Antiques
212 987 8505

Louis XV commode:
Newel Art Galleries, Inc.
(to the trade only)
212 758 1970
www.artresources.com
Louis XV heartback chair:
Frederick P. Victoria & Son
(as above)
Louis XV provincial chest:
Newel Art Galleries, Inc.
(as above)
Louis XV-style magazine table:
Frederick P. Victoria & Son
(as above)
"Charlotte" sofa:
Ashley Manor Furniture
800 582 1401
www.ashleymanorfurniture.com
Umbrella bed:
Designed by Charlotte Moss
Made by Frederick P. Victoria
& Son (as above)

ACCESSORIES

**Collection of Chinese vases,
including pair of turquoise vases:**
Oriental Decorations
212 439 1573
1920s French Aubusson carpet:
F. J. Hakimian
212 371 6900
www.fjhakimian.com
also available from
Mansour
800 540 4707
www.mansoursruggallery.com
Double gourd lamps:
John Boone, Inc.
212 758 0012
Fire screen:
William H. Jackson & Company
212 753 9400
www.wmhjackson.com

**19th-century Japanese
Kakiemon vases:**
John Rosselli International
(as above)

**1950s Italian mirror-backed
sconces:**
John Rosselli International
(as above)
19th-century needlepoint rug:
F. J. Hakimian
(as above)
Palm leaf mirrors:
John Rosselli International
(as above)
**Pillows from antique
Chinese textiles:**
similar new and vintage
fabrics available through
Indigo Seas
310 550 8758
also available from
Virginia di Sciascio
212 794 8807
Porcelain fruits:
Lady Anne Gordon
C.M. Leonard Antiques
203 253 5843
other ceramic fruits available from
B.D. Jefferies
800 954 3004
www.bdjeffries.com
**Silver accessories, including
sterling-silver magnifying lens,
green aventurine magnifying glass,
chrysoprase toad, sterling silver
bell, small silver place-card holder,
pink rhodochrosite salt cellar,
blue lacquer and gold-plated
fountain pen:**
Verdura
212 758 3388
www.verdura.com

Sisal floor covering:
Rosecore Carpets, a division of
F. Schumacher
(see above)
Throws:
Loro Piana
available through fine retailers

From the collection of
Charlotte Moss:
Antique Turkish bed slippers
Bronze turtle
Celadon bud vases
Chinese fruit bowl
Decalcomania lamp
Green bud vases
Rose medallion saucer
White vases

From the collection of
Charlotte Moss:
French 19th century engravings
Water-color portrait of
the Baroness de Rothschild
by Cecil Beaton
Collection of 18th century
French costume engravings

**A COUNTESS'S CHAMBER
ROOM SCHEME DETAILS**
(see pages 40 and 41)

1. *Antique Chinese embroidery*
2. *De Gournay panels/Stourhead/Yellow*
3. *Lady Anne Gordon porcelain melon*
4. *F. Schumacher/Vendome Tassel
   Fringe/Rose and Dove*
5. *F. Schumacher/Ravinia Silk Taffeta/Ecru*
6. *F. Schumacher/Sargent Silk
   Taffeta/Rouge*
7. *F. Schumacher/Fiorella Damask/Sage*
8. *Antique Chinese silk braid*

A BLISSFUL BEDROOM

FABRICS

UPHOLSTERY

Bed canopy:
Colonial Williamsburg
Reserve Collection
F. Schumacher/Palampore
Border/Document

Lining:
Colonial Williamsburg
Reserve Collection
F. Schumacher/Blaikley Fern/Coral
Tiebacks and trim:
Scalamandre
Slipper chair:
Colonial Williamsburg
Reserve Collection
F. Schumacher/Spring Flowers/Blue

Bed linens:
Guirlande D'Ivoire shams and bed set
Rigoletto cashmere throw
Diamond piqué blanket cover
D. Porthault & Co
212 772 3877
www.d-porthault.com
Walls:
Colonial Williamsburg
Reserve Collection
F. Schumacher/Palampore
Border/Document

WINDOW TREATMENTS

Panels:
Colonial Williamsburg
Reserve Collection
F. Schumacher/Palampore
Border/Document
Sheer shades:
Colonial Williamsburg
Reserve Collection
F. Schumacher/Market Square/Linen

FURNITURE

Small side table:
Les Pierre Antiques
212 243 7740
Caned desk chair:
Paterae
212 941 0880
Cushion:
F. Schumacher/Providence
Check/Colonial Red
Chinoiserie cabinet:
Smith Gurney Antiques, Ltd.
802 496 9088
Louis XVI canopy bed:
Niermann Weeks
(as above)
Louis XV writing table:
Objects Plus, Inc.
212 832 3386

LIGHTING

Bouillotte lamp:
Objects Plus, Inc.
(as above)
Harcourt floor lamp:
Vaughan Designs
212 319 7070
www.vaughandesigns.com
Hurricane lamps:
From the collection of
Charlotte Moss

Neoclassical urn lamp:
Niermann Weeks
(as above)

ACCESSORIES

Covered jar, Delft vases:
John Rosselli International
(as above)
Positano urn:
Niermann Weeks
(as above)
Jardinieres:
Cinnamon Gilt
Niermann Weeks
(as above)
Painted brackets:
From the collection of
Charlotte Moss
Bracket clock:
From the collection of
Charlotte Moss
Painted faux tortoiseshell effect:
Osmundo Echevarria
212 868 3029
Rose Tarlow bed tray:
Holly Hunt
212 755 6555
www.hollyhunt.com
Wall to wall carpet:
Aspen/Beige and Brown
Beauvais Carpets
212 759 8580
www.beauvaiscarpets.com
**19th-century English
needlepoint carpet:**
Beauvais Carpets
(as above)

**From the collection of
Charlotte Moss:**
Chinese painted lock box
Crystal-and-gilt beehive ink well
Embroidered place mat, napkin
Eyeglasses
Gilt frame with porcelain painting
Minton porcelain tea set
Opera glasses
Shagreen eyeglass case
Silver pomegranate
Silver tray

A ROOM FOR CONVERSATION

FABRICS

UPHOLSTERY

Jansen banquette:
Scalamandre/Persia Antique
Velvet/Camel
Trim:
Scalamandre Chenille and
Linen Braid
Frame:
J & M Upholstery
718 780 0104
Painted Swedish chair:
Scalamandre/Monochromo
Lampas/Anis
Trim:
Scalamandre gimp and
cushion cord

A BLISSFUL BEDROOM
ROOM SCHEME DETAILS
(see pages 64 and 65)

1. *F. Schumacher/Mandarin Silk Check/Coral Rose*
2. *F. Schumacher/Blaikley Fern/Coral*
3. *F. Schumacher/Palampore Border/Document*
4. *Holland & Sherry/Natural Cashmere/Light Camel*
5. *Holland & Sherry/Natural Cashmere/White*
6. *Antique tassel*
7. *Antique miniature French chair*
8. *F. Schumacher/Spring Flowers/Blue*

Customized slipper chairs:
Garrett Leather/Chatham/Strawberry
Hinson and Co.
212 688 5538
Leather gaufrage:
Pattern: Iris Blotch
(applied to sueded side of leather)
Daniel C. Duross, Ltd.
518 762 1910
Sybaritic armchair:
Front:
Scalamandre/Aquataine/Slate Velvet
Back:
Scalamandre/Turandor Plaid/Blue
Trim:
Antique braid, antique fabric
on arms

WINDOW TREATMENTS

Panel fabric:
Scalamandre/Namtu Faille/
Café au Lait

Piping:
Scalamandre/Raw Silk/Tobacco
Flange:
Scalamandre/Tuscan Faille/Paprika
Silk screening:
Trentino Pattern
Peter Fasano, Ltd.
413 528 6872
www.peterfasano.com

ANTIQUE FURNITURE

Lacquer screen:
Lee Calicchio, Ltd.
212 588 0841
www.leecalicchioltd.com
19th-century Swedish chair:
From the collection of
Charlotte Moss
Pair of George II consoles:
Kentshire Galleries, Ltd.
(to the trade only)
212 673 6644
www.kentshire.com

Regency lacquer chiffonier:
Kentshire Galleries, Ltd.
(as above)
Swedish commode:
Lee Calicchio, Ltd. (as above)

**NEW AND REPRODUCTION
FURNITURE**

Customized slipper chairs:
Crate & Barrel
www.crateandbarrel.com
212 308 0011
Parchment coffee table:
Mary Kuzma Finishing
718 388 8577
Sybaritic chair:
Designed by Charlotte Moss
Made by Frederick P. Victoria & Son
(as above)
Jansen-style banquette:
From the collection of
Charlotte Moss

Round Empire Gueridon table:
Mrs. MacDougall at Hinson & Co.
(to the trade only)
212 688 7754
Square Gueridon table:
Mrs. MacDougall at Hinson & Co.
(as above)

ACCESSORIES

Chinese vase lamps:
From the collection of
Charlotte Moss
Custom shades:
Shades of the Midnight Sun
(to the trade only)
**18th-century French
Aubusson rug:**
Stark Carpets
(as above)
Iron twig jardinieres and lantern:
Dennis & Leen
310 652 0855
www.avenuesartdesign.com

Lippy cat throw:
Dennis Basso
212 794 4500
Pair of footstools:
From the collection of
Charlotte Moss
Pair of giltwood mirrors:
John Rosselli Antiques
(to the trade only)
212 737 2252
Raw silk Hayward pillows:
Crate & Barrel
(as above)
Sang du boeuf lamps:
Christopher Spitzmiller, Inc.
available through Mecox Gardens
www.mecoxgardens .com
Shagreen table lamp:
Sentimento
212 750 3111

ARTWORK

1929 drypoint etching:
Henri Matisse
Ann Kendall Richards, Inc.
212 717 5260
www.artresources.com
1950s _Vogue_ illustration:
René Bouché
Ann Kendall Richards, Inc.
(as above)
1958 fashion photos:
Gleb Derujinsky
Gallagher Gallery
212 473 2404
www.gallaghersfashion.com
Tales of Genji IV 1998 woodcut:
Helen Frankenthaler
Ann Kendall Richards, Inc.
(as above)

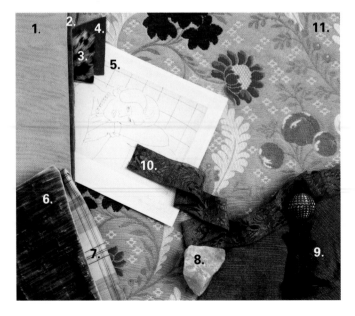

A ROOM FOR CONVERSATION
ROOM SCHEME DETAILS
(*see pages 80 and 81*)

1. Scalamandre/Namtu Faille/
   Café au Lait
2. Scalamandre/Bonard/Coral
3. Lippy cat pelt from Dennis Basso
4. Garrett strawberry leather
5. Matisse etching
6. Scalamandre/Aquataine/Slate Velvet
7. Scalamandre/Turandor Plaid/
   Blue Silk Taffeta
8. Rose quartz
9. Scalamandre/Persia Antique
   Velvet/Camel
   Antique perfume burner
10. Vintage blue and bronze braid
11. Scalamandre/Monochromo
    Lampas/Anis

BUYING GUIDE

A SELECT LIST OF SOME FAVORITE NATIONWIDE RETAILERS AND MAIL-ORDER SOURCES

FOR FURNITURE, ACCENT PIECES, AND HOME DECORATING ACCESSORIES

Anthropologie
800 309 2500
www.anthropologie.com
Window panels, tiebacks,
and hardware

Ballard Design
800 367 2775
www.ballarddesigns.com
Home accessories

B. D. Jefferies
800 954 3004
www.bdjefferies.com
Table linens, leather goods,
and glassware

Chambers
800 334 9790
www.williamssonoma.com
Linens for bed and bath

Crate & Barrel
800 967 6696
www.crateandbarrel.com
Furniture, cushions, accessories

Exposures
800 572 5750
www.exposuresonline.com
Leather journals and photo
organization supplies

Hold Everything
800 421 2285
www.holdeverything.com
Organization for desk and closet

Horchow
877 944 9888
www.horchow.com
Home accessories and linens

Levenger
800 667 8034
www.levenger.com
Desk accessories; library fittings

Le Vivre
800 230 4354
www.vivre.com

Links of London
800 210 0079
www.linksoflondon.com
Personal and desk accessories in silver

Olympus
www.olympusamerica.com
Cameras—essential inspiration-
gathering companions

Pearl River
800 878 2446
www.pearlriver.com
Traditional Chinese pottery, textiles,
and accessories

Pier One
800 245 4595
www.pier1.com
Colorful glassware and tableware

Pierre Deux
888 743 7732
www.pierredeux.com
Classic French table linens; ceramics

Pottery Barn
800 993 4923
www.potterybarn.com
Furniture and decorative
accessories at great value

**The Source Perrier Collection for
Home and Garden**
888 543 2804
www.sourceperrier.com
Furniture, lighting, cashmere throws,
embroidery, and objects for beautiful
table settings

Tiffany & Company
800 843 3269
www.tiffany.com
A classic for silver accessories,
hand-painted porcelain

Wisteria
800 767 5490
www.wisteria.com
Unusual furniture and decorative
accessories; wicker and rattan;
zinc planters and tables

ACKNOWLEDGMENTS

As always, a book is quite a team effort.

I am eternally grateful to everyone who has worked on this book. In my offices here at Charlotte Moss & Company, I'd like to thank Beatrice Dugdale for her organization, diligence, and enthusiasm; Ricky Spears, who has his hand in a little bit of everything; Jessica Everhart for organizing the people, the meetings, the photo shoots, and the cataloguing of chromes and slides, and for securing rights to photos and tracking down photographers—even in Russia; Michelle Canning, who has the greatest "let's get it done" attitude, for taking ownership and managing the process long after it had already started and for her enthusiasm for this project and everything else she works on.

I'd also like to thank my writer, Jennifer Cegielski, who took my notes, asked lots of questions, gave me terrific, balanced insight, and then crafted this text.

Many thanks to dk Design Partners for the layout, design, and production of this book. While Dina Dell'Arciprete has her own company (dk Design Partners, Inc.) with her husband, Kurt, I feel that she is very much a member of the Charlotte Moss team. I am grateful for her "eye"—she sees what I often pass by in my day, and her graphic vision has made her my very much respected Art Director.

And, of course, my thanks extend to the work of the wonderful photographers whose images appear on these pages: Nathan Sayers and Jason Dewey for assorted photos throughout; Feliciano for the photos in "A Feminine Retreat"; Michael Mundy for the photos in "A Countess's Chamber"; Pieter Estersohn for the photos in "A Blissful Bedroom"; and Beatriz DaCosta for the photos in "A Room for Conversation."

I would also like to thank all the teams involved with the execution and seamless operation of the show houses at Kips Bay, and for the American Hospital of Paris for the French Show House. Both of these institutions are the beneficiaries of the teams' efforts and the generosity of designers and their suppliers. I salute all of your efforts, and I look forward to my next opportunity to participate.

And then there is my patient and supportive husband, Barry.
Thank you for always being there.